NFL TEAM STORIES

The Story of the
ARIZONA CARDINALS

By Craig Ellenport

Kaleidoscope
Minneapolis, MN

The Quest for Discovery Never Ends

This edition first published in 2021 by Kaleidoscope Publishing, Inc.

No part of this publication may be reproduced in whole or in part without written permission of the publisher.

For information regarding permission, write to
Kaleidoscope Publishing, Inc.
6012 Blue Circle Drive
Minnetonka, MN 55343

Library of Congress Control Number
2020933363

ISBN
978-1-64519-218-3 (library bound)
978-1-64519-286-2 (ebook)

Text copyright © 2021 by Kaleidoscope Publishing, Inc. All-Star Sports, Bigfoot Books, and associated logos are trademarks and/or registered trademarks of Kaleidoscope Publishing, Inc.

Printed in the United States of America.

FIND ME IF YOU CAN!

Bigfoot lurks within one of the images in this book. It's up to you to find him!

TABLE OF CONTENTS

Kickoff! 4

Chapter 1: Cardinals History 6

Chapter 2: Cardinals All-Time Greats 16

Chapter 3: Cardinals Superstars 22

Beyond the Book 28
Research Ninja 29
Further Resources 30
Glossary 31
Index 32
Photo Credits 32
About the Author 32

KICKOFF!

There are two Red Seas. One is really famous. It's in the Middle East near Egypt. The other is famous in the NFL. It's the name of Arizona Cardinals fans! They wear red and cheer for their favorite team. The Red Sea packs State Farm Stadium for every game. The "Cards" have given their fans lots to cheer for. The team has been playing for more than 100 years—just not in Arizona! Let's dive into the Red Sea with the Cardinals!

Cardinals fans help form the Red Sea.

Chapter 1
Cardinals History

The Cardinals started before the NFL! The Chicago Cardinals football club began in 1898. They played other pro and **amateur** teams.

The NFL began in 1920. The Cardinals were one of the first 14 teams. The Cardinals played

The 1925 Cardinals in action (dark jerseys).

well in the first five seasons. In 1925, they put it all together. Norm Barry was named the new head coach. He led the Cardinals to a record of 11-2-1. That was the best record for any of the 20 teams in the league. The Chicago Cardinals earned their first NFL championship!

FUN FACT
The NFL's first name was the American Professional Football Association. It switched to NFL in 1922.

After 1925, the Cardinals struggled for many years. In 1947, the team added running back Charley Trippi. Trippi was a star in college football. He helped the Cardinals finish 9-3. They went to the NFL Championship Game against the Philadelphia Eagles. Trippi and Elmer Angsman scored two touchdowns each. The Cardinals won, 28-21. The Cardinals were champions again!

The champion 1947 Cards.

The snow-covered 1948 championship game.

In 1948, the Cardinals went back to the NFL Championship Game. They played the Eagles again. A huge snowstorm hit Philadelphia before the game. The players had to run through it! There was only one score in the game. The Eagles scored a touchdown and won 7–0.

In 1960, the Cardinals moved to St. Louis. They played in St. Louis for 28 years. That city was already home to another Cardinals team. It played in Major League Baseball. That's a lot of Cardinals!

The St. Louis Cardinals won the NFC East Division title in 1974 and 1975. They had an excellent offense. The offense was led by QB Jim Hart and running back Terry Metcalf. Fans loved watching this high-scoring team. But the team moved again in 1988. This time the Cardinals went to Arizona!

QB Jim Hart

WHY CARDINALS?

Charles O'Brien ran the Chicago football club in 1901. The team played at Chicago's Normal Field. Its nickname was the Normals. O'Brien bought new jerseys from the University of Chicago. Somebody said the uniform color was maroon. "That's not maroon," said O'Brien. "It's Cardinal red!" Ever since, the team name has been the Cardinals!

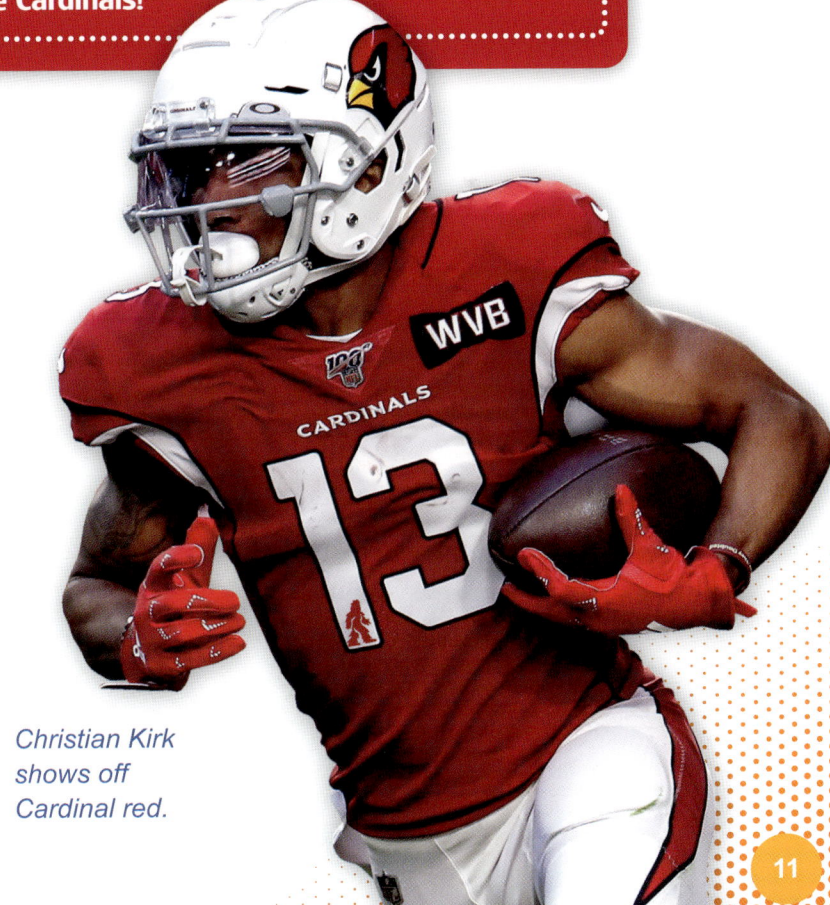

Christian Kirk shows off Cardinal red.

The Cardinals went to the playoffs in 2009. They played the Green Bay Packers in a Wild Card Playoff Game. Kurt Warner threw five touchdown passes. The Cardinals won in overtime, 51-45. It was the highest-scoring playoff game in NFL history!

Arizona made it to the playoffs again in 2015. That team featured a high-scoring offense, too. The Cardinals lost to the Carolina Panthers in the NFC Championship Game.

The Cardinals haven't been back to the playoffs since then. In 2019, they hired a new coach, Kliff Kingsbury. The Cards have a young star in QB Kyler Murray. Arizona's future seems bright!

Kurt Warner lit up the scoreboard against the Packers.

TIMELINE OF THE ARIZONA CARDINALS

1925
1925: The Chicago Cardinals win the NFL Championship.

1947
1947: The Cardinals win the NFL Championship again!

1960
1960: The Cardinals move to St. Louis.

1974
1974: The Cardinals win the NFC East Division.

1988
1988: The Cardinals move to Phoenix, Arizona.

2008
2008: Arizona wins the NFC West Division. The Cardinals lose to the Steelers in Super Bowl XLIII.

2015
2015: The Cardinals finish 13-3 and win the NFC West Division.

2019
2019: Kliff Kingsbury's first year as head coach.

FALLEN HERO

A statue stands outside State Farm Stadium in Glendale, Arizona. It shows one of the Cardinals' players. Pat Tillman was a top defender for Arizona. He hit hard and always gave his best. He got his statue for what he did off the field.

Tillman was a safety for the Cardinals from 1998-2001. The Cardinals offered him a million dollars a year to keep playing. Tillman had other plans. The United States had been attacked on September 11, 2001. Tillman wanted to help fight back. He turned down the Cardinals money. He left the team and the NFL to join the U.S. Army. Tillman was sent to the Middle East. Sadly, in 2004, Tillman was killed in battle. Fans everywhere were inspired by Tillman's bravery.

The Cardinals put up the statue in 2006. They retired Tillman's jersey number. In his memory, no Cardinal will ever wear number 40 again.

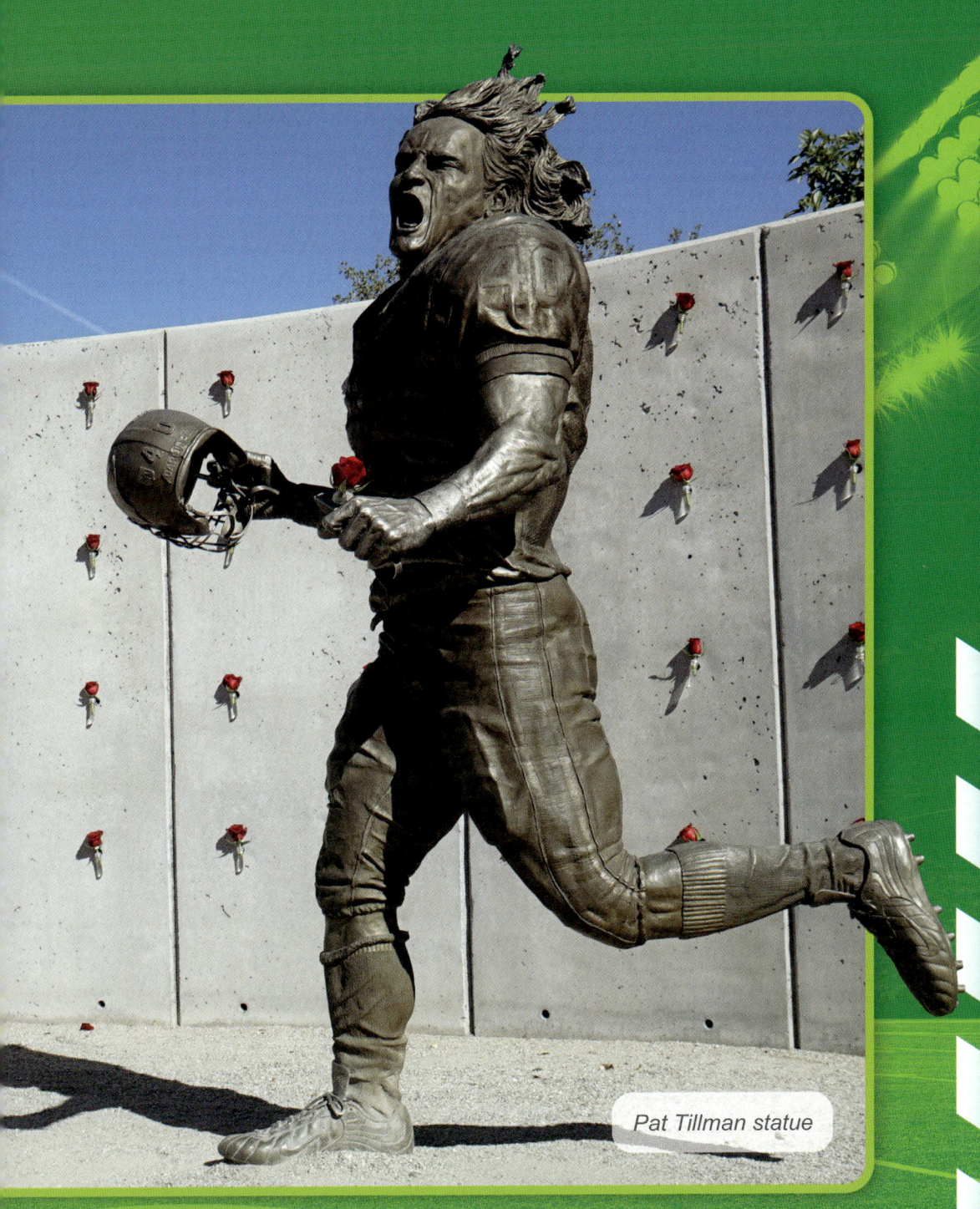
Pat Tillman statue

Chapter 2
Cardinals All-Time Greats

The first Cardinals superstar was running back Ernie Nevers. In 1929, Nevers set an NFL record. It may never be broken. He scored 40 points in one game! Nevers ran for six touchdowns. He also kicked four extra points. Imagine Ezekiel Elliott doing that today! The Cardinals beat the Bears 40–6.

Charley Trippi helped the Cardinals win the 1947 NFL Championship. Trippi was a fast runner. He broke big plays both running and catching the football.

Ollie Matson played for the Cardinals in the 1950s. Matson was a tough runner who was hard to tackle. Matson also returned six kickoffs for touchdowns.

Charley Trippi tries on the Cardinals helmet—yup, no face mask!

In St. Louis, the Cards had two Hall of Fame defensive backs. Larry Wilson was a safety. He was good at **blitzing** the quarterback. He also had 52 career **interceptions**.

From 1969-82, Roger Wherli played cornerback for the Cardinals. Wehrli stuck to receivers like glue. He had 40 interceptions.

Dan Dierdorf was one of the best offensive linemen in NFL history. Dierdorf had brute strength. He was also an excellent athlete. Dierdorf played in six **Pro Bowls** and went on to the Hall of Fame.

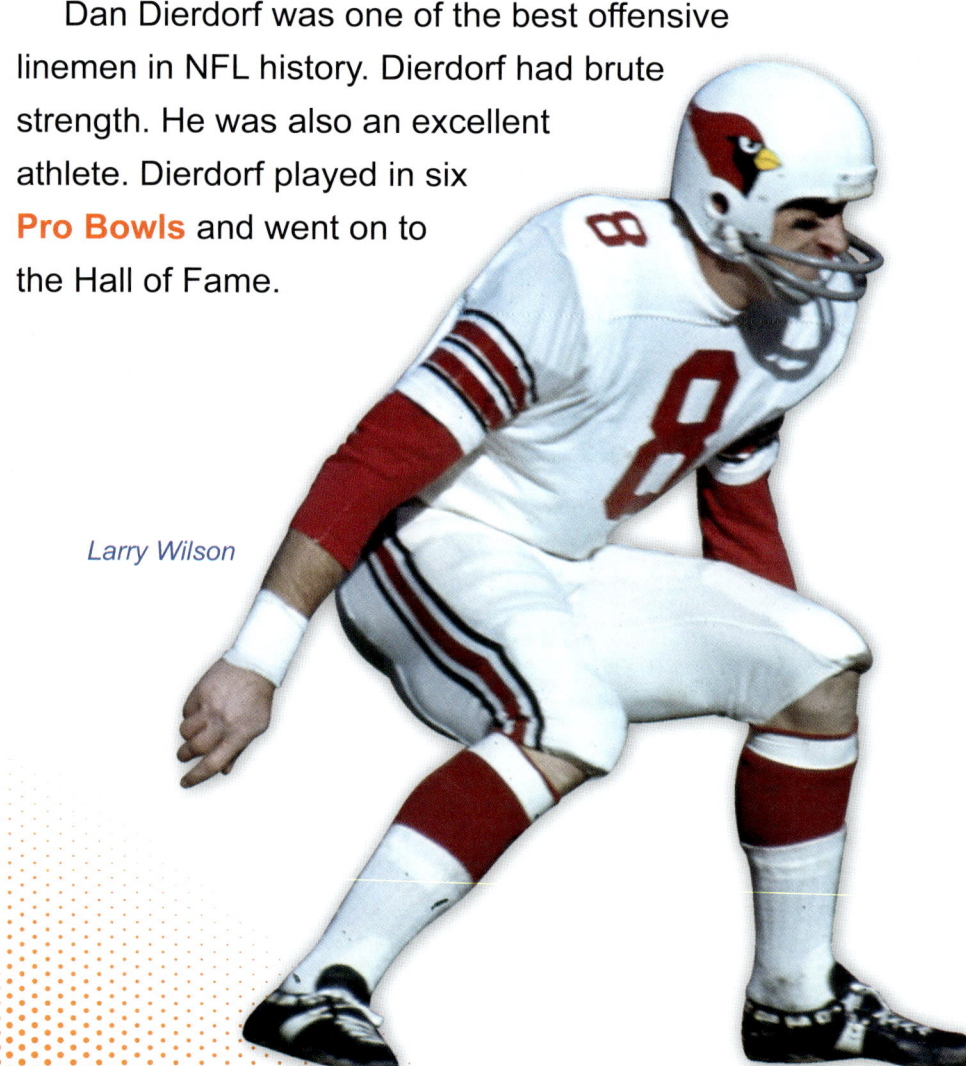

Larry Wilson

Aeneas Williams

In the 1990s, the Cardinals' best player was cornerback Aeneas Williams. Williams had 46 career interceptions. He had blazing speed. When he made a pick, he was a threat to score. Williams returned six interceptions for touchdowns in his career.

Larry Centers was a two-way threat at running back. In 1996, he was the first running back to catch at least 100 passes.

In the 2000s, the Cardinals had success with two quarterbacks. Both had first starred for other teams. In 1999, Kurt Warner won a Super Bowl with the St. Louis Rams. In 2008, Warner led the Cardinals to the Super Bowl.

Carson Palmer was a Pro Bowl QB for the Cincinnati Bengals. With Arizona, he set a team record with 35 touchdown passes in 2015.

Carson Palmer

CARDINALS
RECORDS

These players piled up the best stats in Cardinals history. The numbers are career records through the 2019 season.

Total TDs: Larry Fitzgerald, 120

TD Passes: Jim Hart, 209

Passing Yards: Jim Hart, 34,639

Rushing Yards: Ottis Anderson, 7,999

Receptions: Larry Fitzgerald, 1,378

Points: Jim Bakken, 1,380

Sacks: Freddie Joe Nunn, 66.5

Chapter 3
Cardinals Superstars

Today's Cardinals are a young team. Still, their best player in his 17th season! Larry Fitzgerald is one of the best receivers ever. Only one other receiver has more career catches and yards than Fitzgerald.

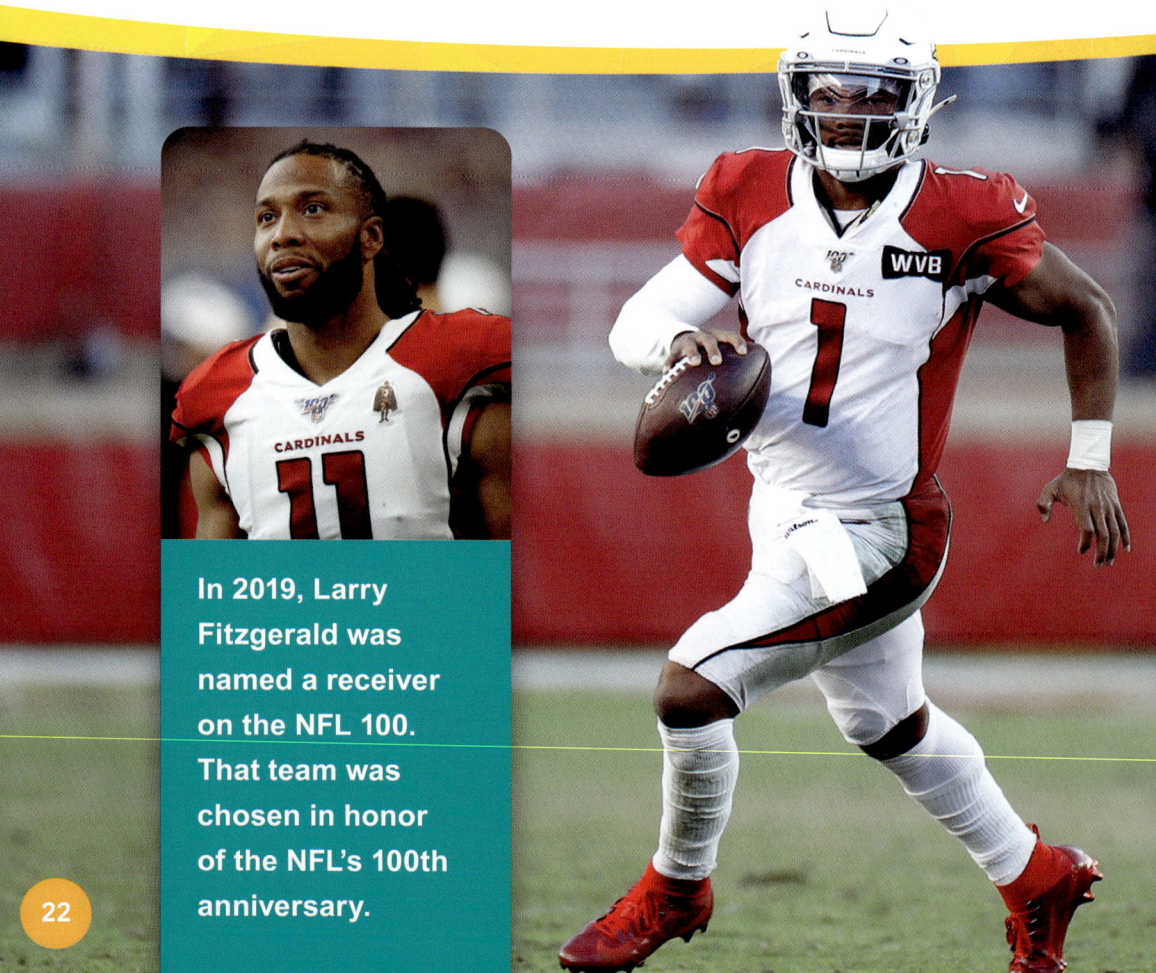

In 2019, Larry Fitzgerald was named a receiver on the NFL 100. That team was chosen in honor of the NFL's 100th anniversary.

Fitzgerald has really helped QB Kyler Murray. The Cardinals **drafted** Murray No. 1 in 2019. As a **rookie**, Murray showed they had made the right choice. He uses his speed and quickness to avoid defenders. Defenses must prepare for his running ability. That makes him even more dangerous as a passer! Murray was named the NFL Offensive Rookie of the Year.

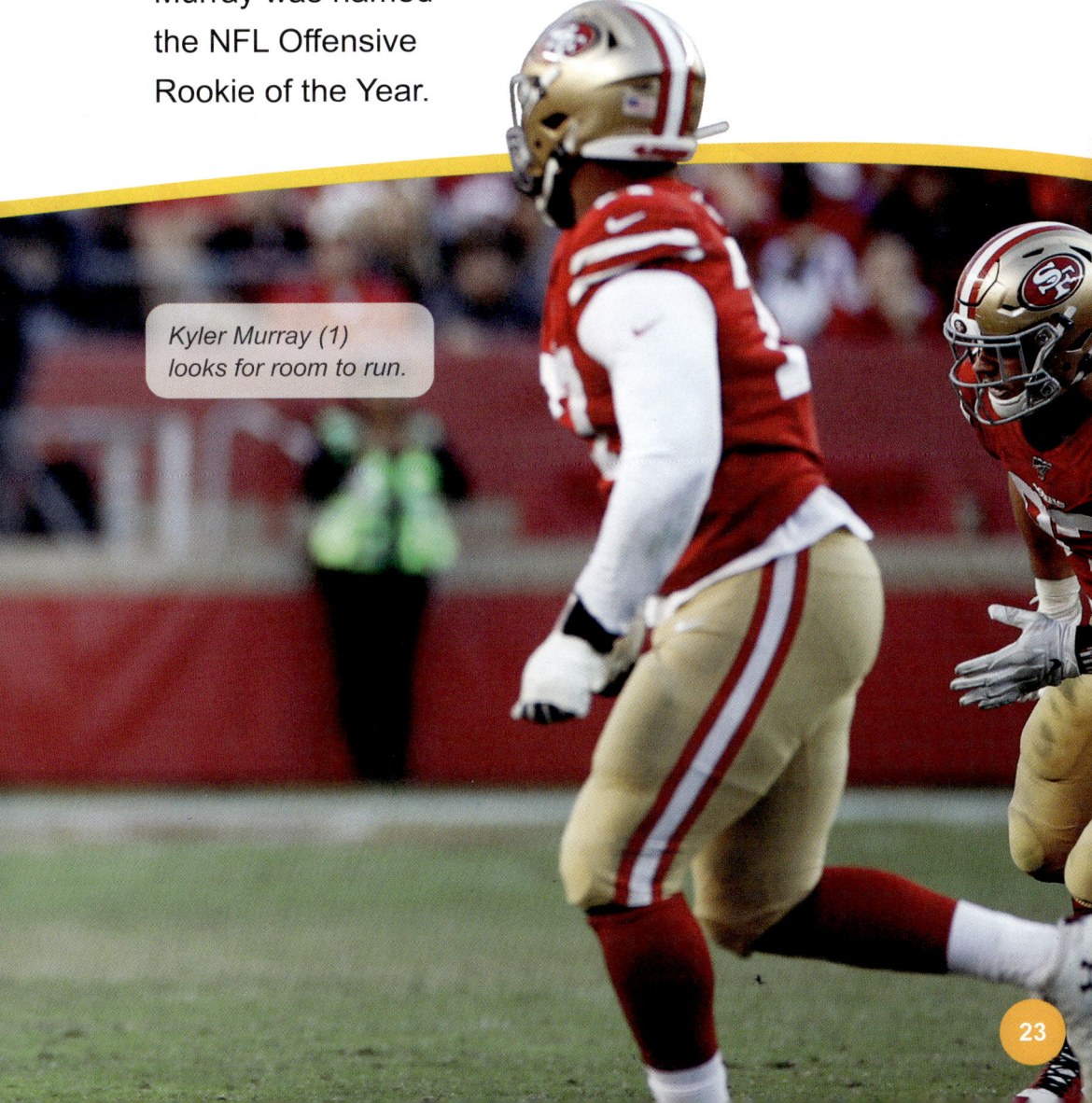

Kyler Murray (1) looks for room to run.

The Cardinals made another big trade in 2020. They got wide receiver DeAndre Hopkins from the Texans. Hopkins made the Pro Bowl four times in Houston. He caught 104 passes in 2019.

DeAndre Hopkins played for Houston from 2013 to 2019.

Kenyan Drake

In 2019, the Cardinals got running back Kenyan Drake. He used to be with the Miami Dolphins. Drake rushed for 817 yards in 2019. He scored seven touchdowns in the season's final three games. Against the Cleveland Browns, he ran for four scores!

Receiver Christian Kirk became one of Murray's favorite targets in 2019. Kirk and Murray played together one year in college.

Chandler Jones

Linebacker Chandler Jones is the leader of the Cardinals defense. Jones' number one job is to **sack** the quarterback. Few players in the league do it better. Jones uses a combination of speed and power. That helps him get around the offensive line. Since joining the Cardinals in 2016, Jones has had 60 sacks. That's almost one sack every game!

Cornerback Patrick Peterson has been to the Pro Bowl eight times. Peterson is one of the fastest players in the NFL. He has 25 career interceptions.

Safety Budda Baker is tough against the pass or the run. Baker led the NFL in 2019 with 104 solo tackles.

On offense and defense, the Cardinals are flying! Will they make the Red Sea keep cheering?

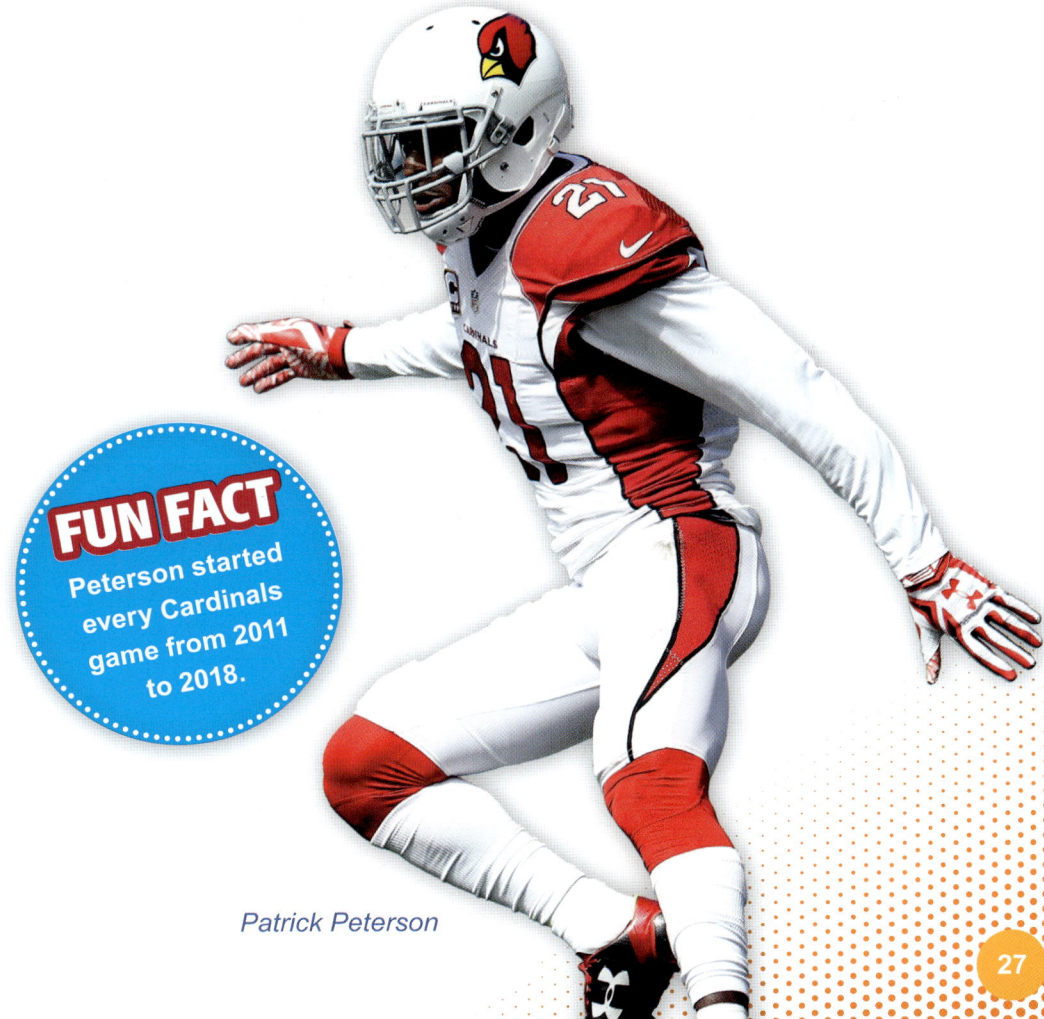

FUN FACT
Peterson started every Cardinals game from 2011 to 2018.

Patrick Peterson

BEYOND THE BOOK

After reading the book, it's time to think about what you learned. Try the following exercises to jumpstart your ideas.

RESEARCH

FIND OUT MORE. Where would you go to find out more about your favorite NFL teams and players? Check out NFL.com, of course. Each team also has its own website. What other sports information sites can you find? See if you can find other cool facts about your favorite team.

CREATE

GET ARTISTIC. Each NFL team has a logo. The Cardinals logo shows a bright red bird head. Get some art materials and try designing your own Cardinals logo. Or create a new team and make a logo for it. What colors would you choose? How would you draw the mascot?

DISCOVER

GO DEEP! As this book shows, Pat Tillman became a hero for his service. Research how other NFL players and sports stars have helped in the military, before or during their careers. How do you think they and Tillman made the choice to serve instead of play?

GROW

GET OUT AND PLAY! You don't need to be in the NFL to enjoy football. You just need a football and some friends. Play touch or tag football. Or you can hang cloth flags from your belt; grab the belt and make the "tackle." See who has the best arm to be quarterback. Who is the best receiver? Who can run the fastest? Time to play football!

RESEARCH NINJA

Visit **www.ninjaresearcher.com/2183** to learn how to take your research skills and book report writing to the next level!

RESEARCH

DIGITAL LITERACY TOOLS

SEARCH LIKE A PRO
Learn about how to use search engines to find useful websites.

FACT OR FAKE?
Discover how you can tell a trusted website from an untrustworthy resource.

TEXT DETECTIVE
Explore how to zero in on the information you need most.

SHOW YOUR WORK
Research responsibly— learn how to cite sources.

WRITE

GET TO THE POINT
Learn how to express your main ideas.

PLAN OF ATTACK
Learn prewriting exercises and create an outline.

DOWNLOADABLE REPORT FORMS

Further Resources

BOOKS

Cooper, Robert. *Great Moments in NFL History*. Mankato, Minn.: North Star Editions, 2019.

Sports Illustrated Kids. *From Then to Wow!* New York: Sports Illustrated Kids, 2014.

Whiting, Jim. *Arizona Cardinals (NFL Today)*. Minneapolis: Creative Paperbacks, 2019.

WEBSITES

FACTSURFER

Factsurfer.com gives you a safe, fun way to find more information.

1. Go to www.factsurfer.com.
2. Enter "Arizona Cardinals" into the search box and click 🔍
3. Select your book cover to see a list of related websites.

Glossary

amateur: unpaid to play sports. All college teams must have amateur players.

blitzing: rushing the quarterback from linebacker or secondary positions. Outside linebacker Chandler Jones is an expert at blitzing.

drafted: chosen during the NFL's annual selection of college players. In 2020, Arizona drafted linebacker Isaiah Simmons in the first round.

interception: a pass caught by the defense. Cornerback Aeneas Williams was one of the NFL's best at making interceptions.

Pro Bowl: the NFL's annual All-Star game. Larry Fitzgerald has been named to 11 Pro Bowls in his career.

retired: stopped playing a pro sport or prevented a jersey number from ever being used again. Kurt Warner retired after five great seasons with the Cardinals.

rookie: a player in his first pro season. Arizona's Kyler Murray was named the NFL Offensive Rookie of the Year in 2019.

sack: a tackle of the quarterback behind the line of scrimmage. Jones was one of the NFL's sack masters in 2019.

Index

Angsman, Elmer, 8
Baker, Budda, 27
Barry, Norm, 7
Carolina Panthers, 12
Centers, Larry, 20
Chicago Cardinals, 6, 7, 8, 9
Dierdorf, Dan, 18
Drake, Kenyan, 25
Fitzgerald, Larry, 22, 23
Green Bay Packers, 12
Hart, Jim, 10
Hopkins, DeAndre, 24
Jones, Chandler, 26
Kingsbury, Kliff, 12
Kirk, Christian, 25
Matson, Ollie, 16
Metcalf, Terry, 10
Miami Dolphins, 25
Murray, Kyler, 12, 23, 25
Nevers, Ernie, 16
Palmer, Carson, 20
Peterson, Patrick, 27
Philadelphia Eagles, 8, 9
Red Sea, 4, 27
St. Louis Cardinals, 10, 18
State Farm Stadium, 4
Tillman, Patt, 14
Trippi, Charley, 8, 16
U.S. Army, 14
University of Chicago, 11
Warner, Kurt, 12, 20
Wherli, Roger, 18
Williams, Aeneas, 19
Wilson, Larry, 18

PHOTO CREDITS

The images in this book are reproduced through the courtesy of: AP Images: 6, 16; Pro Football Hall of Fame 9; David Durochik 10; Mitchell Reibel 12; Gene Lower 14; NFL Photo 18. Focus on Football: 22, 23, 24, 25, 27. Newscom: Larry Radloff/Icon SW 4; Kevin Abele/ Icon W 11; John C. Anderson/UPI 19; Bill Greenblatt/UPI 20; Adam Bow/Icon SW 26. **Cover photo:** Focus on Football.

About the Author

Craig Ellenport, a freelance writer who resides in Massapequa, New York, has written several kids books about the National Football League.